A Free Mind
Ahmed Kathrada's Notebook
from Robben Island

Edited by Sahm Venter

From an idea by Kimberley Worthington

Kathy was, and is, a political animal. But, more than most of his species, he demonstrates the simple fact that political animals are all too human.

– *Dr Neville Alexander*, former Robben Island prisoner

Ahmed Kathrada is the real deal: a fearless activist, who risked his life in the struggle for South Africa's liberation; a humble leader, who worked tirelessly behind the scenes to build a new democracy; and an all around incredible human being, who possesses genuine compassion, real wisdom, and a great sense of humour.

– *Danny Glover*

It is great to know that the elders did not give up hope, and used their time to record our history for our children and future generations to know and read about. Mr Kathrada will be a good ambassador to encourage the other elders to record their stories before they get lost.

– *Farieda Khan-Ricketts*, former MK soldier and
    political prisoner

Our long discussions in the prison library – sometimes taking weeks – our robust but good natured debates. These were important bricks in my personal development.

– *Sbu Ndebele*, KwaZulu-Natal Premier and former
    Robben Island Prisoner

A free spirit in prison, he has chosen to remain outside
the 'prison' of high office in freedom!
– *Sri Gopal Krishna Gandhi*, Governor of West Bengal
  and grandson of Mahatma Gandhi

Ahmed is a person of strong moral stature who, in prison,
led by example as how to survive in the face of adversity.
As he was in charge of communications, one of the
riskiest jobs in the ANC, he received contraband, such as
newspapers, from various sources and often had to hide it
in his cell. He was, therefore, under almost perpetual risk,
but he did the job in a quiet and disciplined manner.
– *Eddie Daniels*, former Robben Island prisoner

Kathy Kathrada exemplifies a value system and a
generation which South Africa is already missing.
He has dedicated his life to service. His continuing
contributions to the making of history and the
documenting of history are considerable.
– *Centre of Memory*, Nelson Mandela Foundation

I was supposed to be your master but instead you
became my mentor.
– *Christo Brand*, former Robben Island and Pollsmoor
  Prison warder

I have tremendous respect for Ahmed Kathrada, who has been at the center of South Africa's liberation struggle and has been an essential guardian of its history. He has worked to ensure that the world will remember Robben Island and the extraordinary people imprisoned there, who stood up at great personal cost and helped shape the future of their nation. He is one of our great heroes, who must never be forgotten.
– *Blair Underwood*

The person you are and the place you occupy in the making of our country's freedom makes you a person through whom so many vest their own lives with meaning.
– *Mac Maharaj*, former Robben Island prisoner

On a tour of Robben Island, Ahmed Kathrada, ex-political prisoner #468/64, took me by the hand and led me into a place so small, I couldn't imagine how it could have held dreams so immense. I crossed not into his prison cell block, but into a sanctuary, a place made sacred by the power of ideas shared and the integrity of lives lived there. He told me 'war stories' of the days inside – painful, ironic, and often quite funny. Comrade Kathy's intelligence and grace transformed my tour of rage and sadness into a walk of redemption and renewal.
– *Alfre Woodard*

A dedicated revolutionary and true freedom fighter.
– *Indres Naidoo*, former Robben Island prisoner

Kathy's power lies in his humility, intelligence and love for his fellow human beings.
– *Amitabh Bachchan*

Ahmed Kathrada's integrity, intelligence and universal views make him one of our living treasures – not only as an important participant in the struggle for freedom, but now also as a narrator of that epochal period in South Africa's history.
– *André Odendaal*, Honorary Professor in History and Heritage Studies, University of the Western Cape

Ahmed Kathrada is a real hero, who walks his talk and teaches by example. He is a humble man, who possesses great courage, compassion, and an unwavering commitment to equality and justice. His memoir gives people around the world an invaluable view into South Africa's recent history and enables us to better understand how one person's goodness can impact a nation.
– *LaTanya and Samuel L Jackson*

I had an opportunity to bask in the warm glow of Ahmed Kathrada during a private tour of Robben Island. Why on earth did this man with such a complex history, and so much on his plate, take the time and the effort to escort a naive red-headed actress from Hollywood on her first jaunt to the continent? There is only one answer. That is Kathy. Non-judgement and generosity of spirit; and I will never forget it.

– *Gillian Anderson*

Ahmed Kathrada is a quiet hero, whose steadfast adherence to the highest ideals helped alter the future of a nation. He is proof that human beings are capable of exceptional goodness even in the most difficult circumstances, and that political power can be wielded with integrity and empathy. By publishing this book of quotes that influenced his thinking and provided him solace during his years in prison, the editor offers readers a unique view into an exceptional mind and expose us to the ideas that helped to shape a great activist leader.

– *Sharon Gelman*, Executive Director, Artists for a New South Africa

I'll never forget going with Ahmed Kathrada and Madiba to Robben Island the day it became a museum. Kathy spoke about the struggles waged for freedom and the unbreakable bonds of friendship forged. The depth of the love these great men have for each other is evident in the wonderful way they tease each other and in their incredible senses of humor. They are true heroes, whose bravery and kindness changed South Africa and set a new standard for the entire world. I have such tremendous respect and love for Kathy and am so grateful he is my friend.

– *Quincy Jones*

By the same author:
Something to Write Home About
(co-edited with Claude Colart)

First published in 2005 by Jacana Media (Pty) Ltd.
10 Orange Street
Sunnyside, 2092
Johannesburg
South Africa

ISBN 1-77009-124-6

Cover design by Disturbance
Set in Janson 11/16
Printed by Pinetown Printers

See a complete list of Jacana titles at www.jacana.co.za

*To Ahmed 'Kathy' Kathrada and all those who
sacrificed their lives in the struggle for democracy in
South Africa. And to the children who inherited
freedom – always remember how we got here.*

Ahmed Kathrada

AHMED KATHRADA WAS BORN in Schweizer-Reneke
in the north-west of South Africa, on 21 August
1929. Inspired by his hero, Dr Yusuf Dadoo, he
became politically active at the age of 11 in
Johannesburg and joined, variously, the Young
Communist League, the Communist Party (and
later the South African Communist Party), the
South African Indian Congress, the African
National Congress and its armed wing, Umkhonto
weSizwe. In the 1940s he met four political activists
who were to further shape his political career and
life – Nelson Mandela, Walter Sisulu, Ismail Meer
and J.N. Singh. 'Kathy', as he is known by his
friends, had his first of many experiences of
imprisonment at the age of 17. He was tried for his
role in the 1952 Defiance Campaign, and in the
1956 Treason Trial. On 11 July 1963 he was arrested
at Lilliesleaf Farm in Rivonia, Johannesburg,
together with Walter Sisulu, Govan Mbeki,
Raymond Mhlaba, Denis Goldberg and Rusty
Bernstein. They were detained for 90 days in

solitary confinement after which they were charged with sabotage and joined on trial by Nelson Mandela, Andrew Mlangeni and Elias Motsoaledi. (Throughout his imprisonment Kathrada, a Muslim, was denied a copy of the Holy Koran, despite one having been provided by his family.)

On 11 June 1964 all the accused, except Rusty Bernstein, were convicted of sabotage and the next day were sentenced to life imprisonment. Kathrada was released from prison on 15 October 1989 and went on to become a Member of Parliament after South Africa's first democratic elections in 1994. He served as President Nelson Mandela's parliamentary counsellor until 1999.

Contents

Foreword

I FEEL DEEPLY PRIVILEGED and honoured at having been asked by Sahm Venter and Kimberley Worthington to provide a foreword to this publication.

Kathy has been my friend and brother, my comrade and political mentor for the past half-century or so and I feel doubly privileged and honoured to write this foreword.

This book is a selection of quotations from hundreds upon hundreds which Kathy recorded in private notebooks which he kept secretly during his imprisonment – which covered 18 years on Robben Island, and seven years in Pollsmoor Prison.

This collection, *A Free Mind: Ahmed Kathrada's Notebook from Robben Island*, had its humble beginnings in 1965, when Kathy was granted permission to do a BA degree in History and Criminology through the University of South Africa. Having received permission from prison officials to study, several months after he first applied, Kathy was entitled to purchase stationery and writing materials, to have the necessary lectures in his possession, to purchase the required text books, and to order the recommended reading for tackling his university assignments.

Camouflaged amongst his university books were ordinary school exercise books which Kathy filled with quotes from books, magazines and often – smuggled newspapers. While the keeping of such notebooks was not officially allowed, over the years Kathy collected and recorded quotations which had captured his imagination. In the process, he filled seven volumes – six while on Robben Island between 1965 and 1982; and the last volume when he was held at Pollsmoor Prison from October 1982 and until his release in October 1989. He chose to undertake a B.Bibliography with a Major in Library Science as it would give him stronger grounds for retaining his position as Librarian of the prison's library – some 5 000 books donated by a Cape Town book store when it closed shop. Kathy and two other prisoners, Sbu Ndebele, now Premier of KwaZulu-Natal and Khehla Shubane, now a businessman, were the Island's 'librarians'. Kathy was the only prisoner from B Section to be allowed access to A Section, which housed, amongst others, the post-Soweto prisoners, to take orders and deliver books. Later on there was mixing between the two sections on weekends.

He and his fellow librarians met once a year to take stock, deliberately taking a few days to count the relatively small number of books so that they could smuggle messages between A and B Sections. He chose his second Major, African Politics, to be able to have access to interesting books.

When Kathy lost his study priviledges – I think it was in the late Seventies, or even early in 1980 or so – all the study materials, as well as the copies of letters he had written to family and friends, and his notebooks of quotations, were confiscated from him and locked in a disused prison cell. Since the prison authorities operated on a skeleton staff over weekends, it often happened that the normal group of warders who were in charge of our section were off duty, and were replaced by warders who normally worked elsewhere, such as in the hospital, or as skippers on the ferry boats.

For Kathy, such a situation opened up certain possibilities, and set him thinking in the direction of 'repossessing' his study material, copies of letters he had written, as well as the volumes of quotations. It was decided that a replacement warder on duty should be approached one weekend and asked to open up the cell, with a view to getting him to allow us to clean it. The unsuspecting warder was rather surprised to find two prisoners willing to volunteer to do cleaning duties, and over a weekend on top of that. He opened the cell and the inevitable followed. Not only was the cell cleaned, but it was also 'cleaned out' of the required material. We stole back all the materials and put them in a couple of cells used as storerooms. When he got back the right to study, he brought everything back to his cell.

The volumes of quotations have been floating around outside prison for the past 16 years. I am glad that Sahm and Kimberley have undertaken the important initiative of publishing the selected quotations, thereby adding greater value to them.

– Laloo 'Isu' Chiba
Lenasia, 2005

Laloo Chiba was a member of the ANC's armed wing, Umkhonto weSizwe, who spent 18 years on Robben Island from 1964 to 1982, for sabotage. He served two terms as an African National Congress Member of Parliament in South Africa's first democratically elected government from 1994 to 1999, and from 1999 to 2004.

Preface

"To be ignorant of what occurred before you were born is to remain always a child". This quote by Cicero is one of hundreds recorded by Ahmed Kathrada during his time in prison. It is in the spirit of these words, that this collection has been compiled.

If it were not for the relatively few published accounts of political detention and imprisonment in South Africa, details of that critical part of our history would be in danger of fading from the collective memory. Kathy's books *Letters from Robben Island*, and his *Memoirs* are amongst those pivotal to the understanding by younger generations of where we come from and what we hope to become as a nation.

This collection, which was conceived by his friend and researcher, Kimberley Worthington, provides a valuable insight into the intellectual and emotional deprivation common to most prisoners and specifically into Kathy's experiences during his extraordinary sacrifice for freedom in South Africa.

Offering a significant source of strength and solace to him in prison, Kathy's choice of quotes parallels his experiences from the early years after he was sentenced to life imprisonment in the Rivonia Trial, to the last seven years spent in Pollsmoor Prison on the outskirts of Cape Town.

He was 35 years of age and had already spent nearly a year in custody when he was sentenced to serve the rest of his life in prison. His physical incarceration, as it turned out, would last for more than a quarter of a century, but he refused to allow his jailers to imprison his mind. Locked away in Robben Island's Maximum Security Prison, he embarked on another struggle – to retain access to the written word he had grown to love as a child.

In the face of adversity a number of prisoners obtained university degrees by correspondence. Kathrada was encouraged and assisted by fellow prisoner, Dr Neville Alexander, to begin university studies and eventually obtained two Bachelors and two Honours degrees. He used the opportunity to collect interesting quotations. Written down in mostly tiny handwriting, to conserve space, and sometimes in italics after another political inmate, Denis Brutus, encouraged him to take up calligraphy, the notebooks provide a portrait of his years in prison. They reflect his pain, anguish and fear, as well as his characteristic optimism, his principles of justice and humanity, and his mischievous sense of humour. He particularly appreciated finding and recording humorous quotations and relating them to his colleagues.

While B Section inmates were permitted subscriptions to the magazines *Huisgenoot* and *Farmer's Weekly*, albeit not always exempt from censorship, their thirst for news and information was so strong that whenever newspapers were encountered, before September 1980 when they were allowed, prisoners used a range of methods to smuggle them. Kathy recalls a day when sawing wood near a rubbish dump close to where prisoners used to empty their night buckets, they came across 15 newspapers. "They were filthy, you know. Wet. And they all came to my cell. I used to spend the whole night going through them ... see what's relevant and start destroying immediately."

This book is divided into four periods: the brutal and oppressive early years on Robben Island; the period from 1971 when a new commanding officer branded his iron-fisted rule on the inmates; the post-Soweto uprising period; and his last years behind bars in Pollsmoor Prison. It has been impossible to include all the quotes he kept, but those selected – consistent with the time periods in which they were recorded and with his own notes retained (in italics) – reflect events both in and outside prison during his incarceration.

It was not intended that this collection would convey the detail of Kathy's life as a political prisoner, which is contained in his own books, but it is hoped that it will transmit a sense of some of his emotions and thoughts during his imprisonment.

– Sahm Venter
  Johannesburg, 2005

Part One

Life Means life
1964 to 1970

AHMED KATHRADA ARRIVED on a windswept and rainy Robben Island on Saturday 13 June 1964 – a bleak and ruthless winter's morning. He and his colleagues had been woken in the dead of night in their communal cell in Pretoria, hours after being sentenced to life imprisonment for sabotage. Handcuffed and shackled, Kathrada to Mbeki, they were ushered onto a military plane and flown, in secret, to the notorious island. Mandela had already begun serving a five-year sentence there (for inciting people to strike and leaving the country without a passport). The others had only heard stories about the cruel and oppressive life which lay in wait. Fingerprinted and processed, exchanging their former identities for prison numbers, insufficient prison clothes and meagre rations, they began a new struggle for dignity. After days in the old prison, they were moved to B Section, where they slept on mats on the floor of their tiny prison cells. Completely isolated from the rest of the prison population, they were locked up for 14 hours a day, forced to do hard labour, forbidden newspapers or radios and allowed to write and receive only one 500-word letter every six months. They hoped that one day they might get out, but they knew only too well that for political prisoners in apartheid South Africa, life meant life.

On 9 May 1966 Bram Fischer, a beloved Rivonia Trial lawyer, was sentenced to life imprisonment for sabotage. Prime Minister H.F. Verwoerd was assassinated on 6 September 1966. Kathrada completed his first BA degree in 1968. For the first time since his imprisonment, he saw a clear view of the night sky when prisoners were evacuated into the courtyard as the island shuddered and shook in response to an earthquake on the mainland in 1969.

Where the mind is without fear and the head is
held high;
Where knowledge is free;
Where the world has not been broken up into
fragments by narrow domestic walls;
Where words come out from the depth of truth;
Where tireless striving stretches its arms towards
perfection;
Where the clear stream of reason has not lost its
way into the dreary desert sand of dead habit;
Where the mind is led forward by thee into ever-
widening thought and action –
Into that haven of freedom, my Father, let my
country awake.
– Rabindranath Tagore, *Gitangali*

If one is truly ready within oneself and prepared
to commit one's readiness without question to
the deed that follows naturally on it, one finds
life and circumstance surprisingly armed and
ready at one's side.
– Laurens Van der Post, *Lost World of the Kalahari*

Fury said to a mouse,
That he met in the house,
'Let us both go to the law:
I will prosecute you –
Come, I'll take no denial;
We must have a trial:
For really this morning
I've nothing to do,'
Said the mouse to the cur,
'Such a trial, dear Sir,
With no jury or judge,
would be wasting our breath.'
'I'll be the judge, I'll be the jury.'
Said cunning old Fury:
'I'll try the whole cause,
and condemn you to death.
– Lewis Carroll, *Alice in Wonderland*

The condition upon which God hath given liberty
to man is eternal vigilance, which condition, if he
breaks, servitude is at once the consequence of his
crime, the punishment of his guilt.
– John Curran, (*speech delivered in Dublin 1790*)

No man is an *Island*, entire of it self;
every man is a piece of the *Continent*,
a part of the *main*; if a *clod* be
washed away by the *sea*, *Europe* is the
less, as well as if a *promontory* were, as
well as if a *manor* of thy friends or of
thine own were; Any man's *death*
diminishes *me*, because I am involved in
Mankind; And therefore never send to know
for whom the bell tolls; It tolls for *thee*.
– John Donne, *Meditation XVII*

(*Victor Hugo makes a donkey meditate and
apostrophize thus*:)
My brother, man if you would know the truth,
We both are by the same dull walls shut in;
The gate is massive and the dungeon strong.
But you look through the keyhole at beyond,
And call this knowledge; yet have not at hand
The key wherein to turn the fatal lock.

Ideas grow quickly when watered by the blood
of martyrs.
– Guiseppe Mazzini

27

(According to Herodotus; the following was the reply given by Xerxes (King of the Persians) to his uncle Artabanus, who tried to dissuade Xerxes from going to war against the Greeks:)

There is reason in what you say, but you ought not to see dangers everywhere or to reckon every risk. If whatever comes up you are going to weigh everything alike, you will never do anything. It is better to be always an optimist and to suffer half the amount of evil, than always to be full of gloomy anticipations and never suffer anything at all. If you attack every proposal made without showing us the right course to follow, you will come to grief as much as those whom you oppose. The scales are evenly balanced. How can a human being know certainly which way they will incline? He cannot. But success generally attends those who wish to act; and it does not attend those who are timid and balance everything. You see the great power which Persia has attained. If my predecessors on the throne had held your views, or without holding them had had counsellors like you, you would never have seen our kingdom become so great. It is by taking risks that they made us what we are. Great things are achieved through great dangers.

– Herodotus

When thee builds a prison, thee had better build
with the thought ever in thy mind that thee and
thy children may occupy the cells.
– Elizabeth Fry

Chorus: (to Electra) A golden wish! Too great,
Daughter, for Heaven to grant
To those of mortal state;
For thought is free. – And yet,
Courage! The double chant
of your reverberant hands
Performs its spell; the powers
of earth arm in your cause;
The loathed oppressor stands
Guilty of broken laws,
The children claim their debt
And cry, 'The fight is ours!'
– Euripides

Poetry is the only verity – the expression of a
sound mind, speaking after the ideal – and not
after the apparent.
– Ralph Waldo Emerson

If you hate a man, don't kill him, but let him live.
– Bhuddist proverb

Other men condemned to exile and captivity, if
they survive, despair; the man of letters may
reckon those days as the sweetest of his life.
– Benjamin Disraeli

I will be as harsh as truth, and as uncompromising
as justice. On this subject I do not wish to think,
or speak, or write with moderation. No! No! Tell a
man whose house is on fire to give a moderate
alarm; tell him to moderately rescue his wife from
the hands of a ravisher; tell the mother to
gradually extricate her babe from the fire into
which it has fallen – but urge me not to use
moderation in a cause like the present. I am in
earnest – I will not equivocate – I will not excuse –
I will not retreat a single inch – and I will be heard.
– William Lloyd Garrison, (*principle leader of the
'Abolitionists' (of slavery) in N. America. Extract
from 'Liberator' (1981), Garrison's paper*)

For the charge, I value it not a rush.
It is the liberties of the people of
England that I stand for. For me to acknowledge a
new court that I have never heard of before, I that
am your King, that should be an example to all the
people of England, to uphold justice and to
maintain the laws – indeed I know not how to do it.
– King Charles I (*at his trial*)

In the struggle which was necessary many guilty
persons fell without the forms of trial, and, with
them, some innocent. These I deplore as much as
anybody and shall deplore some of them to the day
of my death. But I deplore them as I should have
done had they fallen in battle. It was necessary to use
the arm of the people, a machine not quite so blind
as balls and bombs, but blind to a certain degree.
– Thomas Jefferson

Preach not to others what they should eat, but eat
as become you, and be silent.
– Epictetus

Conrad wrote that life sometimes made him
feel like a cornered rat waiting to be clubbed.

Alonzo: (*awaiting execution, in chains*) …Then comes
my death, and in the morning of my day I fall,
which – no, Alonzo, date not the life which thou
hast run by the mean reckoning of the hours and
days which thou has breathed: a life spent worthily
should be measured by a nobler line – by deeds, not
years. Then wouldst thou murmer not, but bless the
Providence which in so short a span made thee the
instrument of wide and spreading blessings to the
helpless and oppressed. Though sinking in decrepit
age, he prematurely falls whose memory records no
benefit conferred by him on man. They only have
lived long, who have lived virtuously.
– Richard Brinsley Sheridan, *Pizarro*

Oh, sirs, I am not guilty. It is not guilt that weighs
upon me, but small sins, innumerable small sins,
sirs – not guilt.
– Mary Blandy, *My Grand Enemy* (*On the eve of her*
execution for parricide.)

Not unto us, but unto the noble army of the
heroic dead be the praise, the glory, and
the laurels of the divine liberty that
purifies the earth, the sea, and the air.
Greater love knoweth no man than the love of
the soldier who lays down his life for
the unborn generations of mankind.
– James Douglas

… fear builds its phantoms which are
more fearsome than reality itself, and
reality when calmly analyzed and its
consequences willingly accepted loses
much of its terror.
– Pandit Nehru, *Discovery of India*

And if I pray, the only prayer
That moves my lips from me,
Is, leave the mind that I now bear,
And give me Liberty.
– Emily Bronte

Matthew Arnold speaks of "the huge Mississippi of
falsehood called History".

We are in some danger of becoming petty in our
study of pettiness; there is a terrible Circean law
in the background that if the soul stoops too
ostentatiously to examine anything it never
gets up again.
– G.K. Chesterton

Public life means not only the supreme enjoyment
of achievement but the continuous agony of
misunderstandings, of differences with friends
and associates, of hideously unfair and wounding
criticisms.
– J.C. Smuts

This man is freed from servile bands,
Of hope to rise, or fear to fall: –
Lord of himself, though not of lands,
And having nothing, yet hath all.
– Sir Henry Wotton

(*Form of oath taking among Shoshone Indians is:*) The
earth hears me. The sun hears me. Shall I lie?

A sure test of greatness in men of action is the
absence of lukewarmness with regard to them.
They are detested or adored.
– Lord Rosebery

Prejudices, it is well known, are most difficult to
eradicate from the heart whose soil has never been
loosened or fertilised by education: they grow
there, firm as weeds among stones.
– Charlotte Bronte, *Jane Eyre*

Damnation, I perceive the divine patience of your
people, but where is their divine anger?
– Galileo

Be calm in arguing: for fierceness makes
Error a fault, and truth discourtesy.
Why should I feel another man's mistakes
more than his sickness of poverty?
In love I should: but anger is not love,
nor wisdom neither, therefore gently move.
– George Herbert

We are the Dead. Short days ago
We lived, felt dawn, saw sunset glow,
Loved and were loved, and now we lie
In Flanders fields.

Take up our quarrel with the foe:
To you from failing hands we throw
The Torch; be yours to hold it high.
If ye break faith with us who die
We shall not sleep, though poppies grow
In Flanders fields.
– Major John McCrae (*1st World War*)

When the house of a great one collapses
many little ones are slain.
Those who had no share in the good fortunes
of the mighty
Often have a share in their misfortune.
The plunging wagon
drags the sweating oxen down with it
into the abyss.
– Bertold Brecht, *The Caucasian Chalk Circle*

… a man who accepts his religion without examining it is like an ox which allows itself to be harnessed.
– Voltaire

Daylight eases the fears and the perplexity of man, and most often it is like a balm and a benediction … there are certain categories of human beings who do not welcome the light of day. A prisoner hugs the night, which is a robe to warm and protect him and comfort him, and daylight brings no cheer to a condemned man. But most often, daylight washes out the confusion of the night.
– Howard Fast, *Spartacus*

Blanqui drilled his body to subjugation to his grand conscience and his noble passions, and commencing as a young man, broke with all that sybaritish in modern civilization. Without the power to sacrifice self, great ideas will never bear fruit.
– Louis Michel, *at the funeral of Blanqui 1881*

Lo! In that house of misery
A lady with a lamp I see.
– Henry Wadsworth Longfellow, *on Florence Nightingale*

If corporal punishment were the highest
emanation of educational wisdom, I should have
been a paragon.
– Auguste Bebel

… neither history, nor fable have ever yet ventured
to record an instance of any one, who, by force of
argument and reason, hath triumphed over
habitual avarice.
– Henry Fielding, *Tom Jones*

…everyone should be allowed to get to heaven in
his own way.
– Frederick the Great of Prussia (*1740 – 1786*)

Creon: No other touchstone can test the heart
of man,
The temper of his mind and spirit, till he be tried
In the practice of authority and rule.
For my part, I have always held the view,
And hold it still, that a king whose lips are sealed
By fear, unwilling to seek advice, is damned
And no less damned is he who puts a friend
Above his country ...
– Sophocles

Leve fit, quod bene fertur onus. (*A burden becomes lighest when it is well borne*)

Marriage has many pains but celibacy has no
pleasures
– Dr Johnson, *celebrated judgement in Rasselas*

Men outlive their love, but they don't outlive the
consequences of their recklessness.
– George Eliot (*Mary Anne Evans*)

On the other side of this agony we will yet do
many happy things together.
(*Not exact quotation – from 'Dark Without Sorrow' by
Sarah Jackson. Collection of love letters between her
and her husband, Steven Jackson, Dramatic Director of
the British Council, who was in hospital, dying of
throat cancer. 1960*)

...Pavel, the lonely bachelor, was just
entering on that infinite twilight
period of regrets that are akin to hopes,
and hopes which are akin to regrets,
when youth is over and old age has not yet come.
– Ivan Turgenev, *Fathers and Sons*

In prosperity you cannot always tell a true friend.
But in adversity you cannot mistake an enemy.
– Eccelesiasticus (*Jerusalem Bible*)

A soft answer turneth away wrath.
– Proverbs

(*The Countess*) had always observed that she got on better with clever women than with silly ones like herself; the silly ones could never understand her wisdom, whereas the clever ones – the really clever ones – always understood her silliness.
– Henry James, *Portrait of a Lady*

There is no duty so much underrated as the duty of being happy. By being happy we sow anonymous benefits upon the world, which remain unknown benefits upon the world, which remain unknown even to ourselves, or when they disclosed, surprise nobody so much as the benefactor.
– Robert Louis Stevenson

The condemned social order has not been built up on paper and ink, and I don't fancy that a combination of paper and ink will ever put an end to it, whatever you may think... (*the bomb maker, i.e. the professor*)
– Joseph Conrad, *The Secret Agent*

We are only wood, carved by the knife of
circumstances.
– Olive Schreiner

… that fellow hasn't virtue enough to be faithful
even to his own villainy.
– Richard Brinsley Sheridan, *School for Scandal*

Who was the moral man? Still more pertinently,
who was the moral woman? The beauty or
ugliness of a character lay not only in its
achievements, but in its aims and impulses; its true
history lay, not among things done, but among
things willed.
– Thomas Hardy, *Tess of the D'Urbervilles*

And not by eastern windows only,
when daylight comes, comes in the light;
In front the sun climbs slow, how slowly,
But westward, look, the land is bright.
– Arthur Hugh Clough

I dislike Shakesperian themes involving Kings,
Queens, august people and their honour. In my
pursuit for bread and cheese, honour was seldom
trafficked in. I cannot identify myself with a prince's
problems. Hamlet's mother could have slept with
everyone at court and I would still feel indifferent
to the hurt it would have inflicted on Hamlet.
– Charles Chaplin, *My Autobiography*

Though I eat coarse rice and drink only water,
though my bent arm is my pillow, happiness may
yet be mine, for ill-gained wealth and empty
honours are only floating clouds.
– Confucius

The unique aim of human existence on earth lies
neither in Heaven nor in Hell, but only in
carrying to its highest perfection the humanity
which we bear within us.
– Desiderius Erasmus

"Next to love" said Raoul "revenge is possibly the most exalted emotion. However, it must be subtle in order to be completely satisfying".
– Liam O'Flaherty, *Land*

And life is colour and warmth and light.
And a striving evermore for these;
And he is dead, who will not fight;
And who dies fighting has increase.
– Julian Grenfell, *Into Battle*

If we work upon marble, it will perish;
if we work upon brass; time will efface it;
if we rear temples, they will crumble into dust;
but if we work upon immortal minds,
if we imbue them with principles,
with the just fear of God and love of our
fellow men, we engrave on those tablets
something which will brighten all eternity.
– Daniel Webster

Some men see things as they are and say why?
I dream of things as they never were and say
why not?
– Robert Kennedy

Build me a land where skin (colour) does not count
Only your understanding.
When no goat-face in a parliament can haunt
And keep things permanently verkramp
When I can love you
Lie next to you on the grass without the
Church's blessing.
When at night with guitars we can sing together
with gifts of flowers.
When I am not willed to feed you with poison
As a strange bird in my nest
When no divorce court
Will blind our children's eyes
When Black and White hand in hand
Can bring peace a love
In my land.
– Antjie Krog (*17. Kroonstad Std (10). Translated
from Huisgenoot magazine*)

[Antjie Krog became an anti-apartheid activist and an internationally acclaimed writer and poet. At the FNB Stadium in Soweto, at a rally to welcome Kathrada and his colleagues after their release from prison in October 1989, he read her poem to the crowd to illustrate how in prison it made him realise that some thinking had changed.]

Often it is a clock, for a clock is not a dead thing, it recollects the past, it has been ticking through the past, it is ticking now and looks forward to times ahead. A clock lives in the present but it lives in the past and in the future too. It is the ideal present, for it has the freedom of Time's three dimensions. Present … present … did the two words come from the same root?
– L.P. Hartley, *The Betrayal*

… the old year was preparing, like an ancient philosopher, to call his friends around him, and amidst the sound of feasting and revelry to pass gently and calmly away.
– Charles Dickens, *Pickwick Papers*

Part Two

A New Dispensation
(1971 to 1975)

A PAUSE IN THE YEARS of brutality was shattered by the advent of a new commanding officer, Piet Badenhorst. On the night of Friday 28 May 1971 a group of warders, many of them drunk, stormed into B Section after having severely assaulted the common law prisoners. They forced Kathrada and his colleagues to strip naked and to face the wall while they searched their cells. Claiming to be looking for contraband, their fury essentially stemmed from the fact that the prisoners were on a hunger strike. When Govan Mbeki, the oldest of the Rivonia Trialists, collapsed, the assailants panicked and withdrew. Perhaps in an unconscious response to this vicious regime, and the passing away of his mother the following year, Kathrada's notebooks took on a more gloomy aspect and, at times, began to reflect on cruelty, and even death.

When he found quotations the authorities regarded as 'undesirable' such as those of Karl Marx and Vladimir Lenin, he disguised them and, in some cases, changed the authors' names. Marx and Engels became 'M&E' and Lenin was referred to by his first names: Vladimir Illych. Words like 'force' and 'prison' were abbreviated.

Kathrada spent six months in solitary confinement as punishment for trying to smuggle a note to Andimba Toivo Ja Toivo of the South West People's Organisation (SWAPO). The only reading matter he was permitted was a Bible, and a copy of Thomas Mann's *Magic Mountain* was smuggled in to him. He noted some Biblical references in German and isiXhosa. At the time Dr Neville Alexander had been teaching him German, while Mbeki and Jackson Fuzile were helping him learn isiXhosa.

Kathrada registered for a second degree, in African Politics and Library Science. On 8 May 1975 Bram Fischer died of cancer after being released from prison to his brother's house in Bloemfontein.

But we get accustomed to mental as well as bodily
pain, without, for all that, losing our sensibility to it.
It becomes a habit of our lives as we cease to imagine
a condition of perfect ease as possible for us. Desire
is chastened into submission, and we are contented
with our day when we have been able to bear our
grief in silence and act as if we were not suffering.
– George Eliot, *Adam Bede*

Fear stupefies but it also teaches.
– Anon

We had a foreboding of the night that was in store
for us. The damp autumn cold struck through our
blankets, our shirts, and our skin. All of us felt
how ruthlessly and fearfully outward powers could
strike to the very core of man, but at the same
time we felt that at the very core there was
something that was unassailable and inviolable.
– Anna Seghers, *The Seventh Cross*

Odent, dum Metuant. (*let them hate, provided they fear*)

Fear of danger is ten thousand times more terrifying than danger itself when apparent to the eyes; and we find the burden of anxiety greater, by much, than the evil we are anxious about.
– Daniel Defoe, *Robinson Crusoe*

F...ce is the midwife of every old society pregnant with a new one.
– *M & E. [Marx and Engels are the authors and Kathrada abbreviated the first word 'force'.]*

To secure ourselves against defeat lies in our own hands, but the opportunity of defeating the enemy is provided by the enemy himself.
– Sun Tzu (*5th century BC Chinese military sage*)

When people in power fail to reach a captive's mind,
to bend it to their will, they try to get at it through
the body,
when they still fail, they mutilate the body.
– Vinoba Bhave

Weapons are disastrous implements, no tools for a
noble being. Only when he cannot do otherwise,
does he make use of them. Quiet and peace are for
him the highest. He conquers, but he knows no
joy in it. He who would rejoice in victory would
be rejoicing in murder. At the victory celebration,
the general should take his place as is the custom
at funeral ceremonies. The slaughter of human
beings in great numbers should be lamented with
tears and compassion. Therefore should he, who
has conquered in battle, bear himself as if he were
at a festival of mourning.
– Lao 'Tse (*Chinese thinker 6 BC*)

Misfortune is the only true international currency
the world has ever had.
– Max Wylie, (*Readers' Digest 11th November 1971*)

When future generations read the history of our
era, maybe they will consider us the last of the
barbarians, for we have perfected the means
of killing while of the art of living we know
very little.
– Franklin D. Roosevelt

Prometheus:
See with what outrage
Racked and tortured
I am to agonize
For a thousand years!
See this shameful prison
Invented for me
By the new master of the gods!
I groan in anguish
For pain present and pain to come:
When shall I see rise
The star of my deliverance?
– Aeschylus

When in doubt, to fight is always to err on the
side of right.
– Lord Horatio Nelson

.... my soul
Is sick of public turmoil – ah! Most sick
of the vain effort to redeem a race
Enslav'd because degenerate; lost to hope,
Because the virtue lost – wrapp'd up in self,
In sordid avarice, luxurious pomp,
And proflegate intemperance – a race
Fierce without courage; abject and yet proud;
And most licentious, tho' most far from free.
– John Thelwell

(Thelwell was a friend of Wordsworth and Coleridge,
a supporter of Reform of the seaman's cause – hunted
by the law, he wrote this after being forsaken by
Wordsworth and Coleridge.)

"Ah, because you have suffered is the one reason
why you should never make others suffer," said
Brother Andre to Madam War. "Only the small
and the mean retaliate for pain. You, Madam, are
too high for it. ... And of what meaning is
suffering, if it does not teach us, who are the
strong, to prevent it for others? We are shown
what it is, we taste the bitterness, in order to stir

us to the well to cast it out of the world. Else this earth itself is hell."
– Pearl Buck, *Pavilion of Women*

Exhaustion of the bodily strength does not necessarily exhaust the will. Faith is only a secondary power; the will is the first. The mountains which faith is proverbially said to move are nothing besides that which the will can accomplish. All that Gillia lost in vigour he gained in tenacity. The destruction of the physical man under the oppressive influence of that wild surrounding sea and rock and sky seemed only to reinvigorate his moral nature.
Gillia felt no fatigue; or rather, would not yield to any. The refusal of the mind to recognize the failings of the body is in itself an immense power...
He endured all this suffering without any other thought than is comprised in the word 'Forward'. His work flew to his head; the strength of the will is intoxicating. Its intoxication is called heroism.
– Victor Hugo, *Toilers of the Sea*

Hecabe: ... you are a low and loathsome breed, all you who grasp at popular honours! Who without a thought betray your friends, for one phrase that will gratify a mob!
– Euripides

Creon:
But charged behind my back on blind suspicion
I will not be. To slur a good man's name
with baseless slander is one crime – another
is rashly to mistake bad men for good.
Cast out an honest friend, and you cast out
Your life, your dearest treasure. Time will teach
The truth of this; for time alone can prove
The honest man; one day proclaims the sinner.
– Sophocles

There is no evil that does not bring good.
– Latin American 'Dicho' (proverb)

... it takes all the running you can do, to keep in the same place. If you want to get somewhere else, you must run twice as fast ...
– Lewis Carroll, *Through the Looking Glass*

… I'm known from Baffin's Bay to Terra del Fuego as 'Bad-Luck' Kearny. And I'm it. Everything I get into goes up in the air except a balloon. Every bet I ever made I lost except when I coppered it. Every boat I ever sailed on sank except the submarines. Everything I was ever interested in went to pieces except a patent bombshell that I invented. Everything I ever took hold of and tried to run I ran into the ground except when I tried to plough… That Saturn, the star that presides over bad luck and evil and disappointment and nothing doing and trouble. I was born under that star…

– O. Henry, *Phoebe*

O house ravaged and maimed!
How can I cross your door?
How can I see you without hate and dread,
Anguish that will not cease?
Earth has for me no way, no room.
What can I say? All language is too poor!
If only I were dead!
A crushing fate has claimed
My life from my mother's womb.
How happy the dead are! Theirs is the peace.

Theirs the dark home I envy and desire.
The sunlight wakes no pleasure in my eyes,
My foot treads the firm earth and feels no joy;
So dear a life was pledged for mine,
Till death with a robber's hand
Seized his unlawful prize and lodged her on the
unseen land.
– Euripides

I know too well what are the sufferings and
difficulties of human life, to wish to take from
anyone convictions which may comfort them.
– Emile Littre (*French Philosopher referring to his
wife's crucifix.*)

It is almost a definition of a gentleman to say he is
one who never inflicts pain.
– Cardinal Newman, *The Idea of a University
Defined (1873)*

History is almost always written by the victors and
conquerors and gives their view.
– Pandit Nehru, *Discovery of India*

Love, it is said, is blind. But hatred is as bad ...
Love, too, may easily die – from a surfeit or a
famine. Hatred never dies; it only sleeps ...
– H.S. Merriman, *Barlasch of the Guard*

Was I sleeping while all the others suffered? Am I
sleeping now? Tomorrow, when I wake, or think I
do, what shall I say of today? ... In all that, what
truth will then be?
– Samuel Beckett, *Waiting for Godot*
(expressing the mood of the '50s)

I grumbled because I had no shoes until I met a
man who had no feet.
– Chinese proverb

When the world possesses Reason, race
horses are reserved for hauling dung
When the world is without Reason, war
horses are bred in the common.
– Tao Te Ching

A dog starved at his master's gate
Predicts the ruin of the State.
– William Blake, *Auguries of Innocence*

First think, then act, then – if you must – speak.
– Arab proverb

It is not until a task is fairly grappled with its
difficulties and perils become fully manifest. There
is nothing like making a commencement for making
evident how difficult it will be to come to an end.
Every beginning is a struggle against resistance.
The first step is an exorable undeciever. A difficulty
which we come to touch pricks like a thorn.
– Victor Hugo, *Toilers of the Sea*

*[The following Biblical references were noted
during Kathrada's six month spell in solitary
confinement. He was consistently refused
access to the Holy Koran throughout his
imprisonment.]*

Greater love hath no man than this, that a man lay
down his life for his friends.
– John, 15 (13)

For it is written in the law of Moses, thou shalt
not muzzle the mouth of the ox that treadeth out
the corn.
– Corinthians, 9 (9)

Judge not, that ye be not judged.
For what judgement ye judge, ye shall be judged:
and with what measure ye mete, it shall be
measured to you again.
And why beholdest thou the mote that is in thy
brother's eye, but considerest not the beam that is
in thine own eye?
– (*Christ's sermon*) Matthew, 7 (1,2, and 3)

And he answered, Fear not: for they that be with
us are more than they that be with them.
– Prophet Elisha. II Kings, 6 (16)

Fear none of those things which them shall suffer:
behold, the devil shall cast some of you into
prison, that ye may be tried;
And ye shall have tribulation ten days: be thou
faithful unto death, and I will give thee a crown
of life.
– Revelations, 2 (10)

Knowest thou not this of old, since man was
placed upon earth,
That the triumphing of the wicked is short, and
the joy of the hypocrite but for a moment?
– Job, 20 (4 and 5)

And now men see not the bright light which is
in the clouds: but the wind passeth, and
cleanseth them.
Fair weather cometh out of the north.
– Job, 37 (21 and 22)

I will lift up mine eyes unto the hills, from whence
cometh my help.
– Psalm 121

We are troubled on every side, yet not distressed;
we are perplexed, but not in despair;
Persecuted, but not forsaken; cast down, but
not destroyed.
– II. Corinthians, 4 (8 and 9)

They that sow in tears shall reap in joy.
– Psalm 126

When the righteous are in authority, the people
rejoice: but when the wicked beareth rule, the
people mourn.
– Proverbs, 29 (2)

Blessed are they which do hunger and thirst after
righteousness: for they shall be filled.
– (*Christ's sermon on the mount*) Matthew, 5 (6)

The 'amen' of nature is always a flower.
– Oliver Holmes

So long as we are, death is not; and where death is present, we are not.
– Thomas Mann, *The Magic Mountain*

"Laughter is one of the human being's points of superiority over the beast," said Petronius to Nero. "Consequently Vitellius has no other argument whereby to prove to us that he is not simply and soley a pig."
– Henryk Sienkiewicz, *Quo Vadis*

I have heard … that the sense of being well-dressed gives a feeling of inward tranquillity which religion is powerless to bestow.
– Ralph Waldo Emerson

Keep your eyes wide-open before marriage, half-shut afterwards.
– Benjamin Franklin

Come, fill the Cup, and in the Fire of Spring,
The Winter Garment of Repentance fling:
The Bird of Time has but a little way
To fly – and Lo! The Bird is on the wing.
– Rubayat of Omar Khayyam

A great nation is a nation which produces
great men.
– Benjamin Disraeli

In the fields of observation, chance only favours a
mind which is prepared ...
– Louis Pasteur (*from 'The Life of Louis Pasteur' –
Rene Vallery-Radot, translated Mrs R.L. Devonshire*)

It is only about things that do not interest one that
one can give a really unbiased opinion, which is no
doubt the reason why an unbiased opinion is
always valueless.
– Oscar Wilde

Truth, Sir, is a great coquette; she will not be
sought with too much passion, but often is most
amenable to indifference. She escapes when
apparently caught, but gives herself up if patiently
waited for; revealing herself after farewells have
been said, but inexorable when loved with too
much fervour.
– Ernest Renan

Nihil actum, si quid agendum (*nothing has been
accomplished if there is still something to be done*)

The law doth punish man or woman
That steals the goose from off the common,
But lets the greater felon loose,
That steals the common from the goose.
– Anon (*18ᵗʰ century – group areas act!!*)

Treason doth never prosper; what's the reason?
Why if it prosper, none dare call it treason.
– Sir John Harrington, *A leilia (1613)*

Our Lord who art in the treasury, whatsoever be thy name, thy power be prolonged, thy will be done throughout the empire, as it is in each session. Give us our usual sops, and forgive us our occasional absences on divisions; as we promise not to forgive those who divide against thee. Turn us not out of our places; but keep us in the House of Commons, the land of Pensions and Plenty; and deliver us from the People. Amen.
– William Hone (*satirist, on George III's men in Parliament. Hone was tried for sedition 3 times in 3 days – and acquitted*)

Men are a dear and wonderful tribe and they often make great husbands and fathers, but we must face the fact that genetically they are the weaker sex. The female of the species, almost any species, is sturdier than the male from infancy to death.
– Dr Estelle Ramey (*professor and endocrinologist, USA*)

He who is contented with being contented will always be contented.
– Chinese proverb

"I had killed so many men. I had been applauded for killing them, promoted for killing them, given medals for killing them; but don't let any fool tell you there's no difference between killing in peace and war. In three seconds after I had killed that man I knew the difference. I knew that I had killed one man too many".
– Oliver Essex (*after robbing and murdering Lupton*)

To a visiting stranger who drank down a glass of extra special brandy in one gulp, Talleyrand explained how one should behave in the presence of certain works of art: "You take your glass in the palms of your hands, and warm it. Then shake it gently, with a circular movement so that the liquid's perfume is released. Then, raise the glass to the nose and breathe deeply."
"And then, my lord?"
"And then, sir, you may place the glass on the table and talk about it."
– (*Readers' Digest May 1972*)

Bread has no sorrow for me, and water no affliction. But to shut me from the light of the sky and the sight of the fields and flowers; to charm my feet so that I can never again ride with the soldiers nor climb the hills; to make me breathe foul damp darkness, and keep from me everything that brings me back to the love of God when your wickedness and foolishness tempt me to hate Him: all this is worse than the furnace in the Bible that was heated seven times. I could do without my warhorse; I could drag about in a skirt; I could let the banners and the trumpets and the knights of soldiers pass me and leave me behind as they leave the other women, if only I could still hear the wind in the trees, the larks in the sunshine, the young lambs crying through the healthy frost, and the blessed, blessed church bells that send my angel voices floating to me on the wind. But without these things I cannot live; and by your wanting to take them away from me, or from any human creature, I know that your counsel is of the devil and that mine is of God.

– Joan of Arc, *St Joan*

… after long study and experience I have come to these conclusions, that: (1) all religions are true, (2) all religions have some error in them, (3) all religions are almost as dear to me as my own Hinduism. My veneration for other faiths is the same as for my own faith. Consequently the thought of conversion is impossible… Our prayer for others ought never to be: 'God! Give them the light thou hast given to me!' but 'Give them all the light and truth they need for their highest development.'
– Mahatma Gandhi (*at the Federation of International Fellowships – 1928*)

India is a "land of dreams and romance, of fabulous wealth and fabulous poverty, of splendour and rags, of palaces and hovels, of famine and pestilence … the country of a hundred tongues, of a thousand religions, and two million gods, mother of history; grandmother of legend and great grandmother of tradition."
– Mark Twain (*1895*)

Let us do nothing for a few years except live.
– Charles-Maurice de Talleyrand (*1795*)

… and so there ain't nothing more to write about, and I am rotten glad of it, because if I'd a knowed what a trouble it was to make a book I wouldn't a tackled it and ain't a going to no more. But I reckon I got to light out for the Territory ahead of the rest, because Aunt Sally she's going to adopt me and sivilize me, and I can't stand it. I been there before.
– Mark Twain, *Huckleberry Finn*

Grow old along with me.
The best is yet to be.
– Browning

No man is the whole of himself; his friends are the rest of him.
– H.E. Forsdick (*Readers Digest December 1972*)

Oedipus:
Time, time, my friend,
Makes havoc everywhere; he is invincible.
Only the gods have ageless and deathless life;
All else must perish. The sap of earth dries up,
Flesh dies, and white faith withers, falsehood
blooms,
The spirit is not constant from friend to friend,
From city to city; it changes, soon or late;
Joy turns to sorrow, and turns again to joy.
Between you and Thebes the sky is fair; but Time
Has many and many a night and day to run
On his uncounted course; in one of these.
– Sophocles

People who have wild ideas about how to run the
earth ought to start with a small garden.
– Readers Digest December 1972

Time seems to change its nature in pr..son *[prison]*. The present hardly exists for there is an absence of feeling and sensation which might separate it from the dead past. Even news of the active, living and dying world outside has a certain dreamlike unreality, an immobilitity and an unchangeableness as of the past. The outer objective time ceases to be, the inner and subjective sense remains but at a lower level, except when thought pulls it out of the present and experiences a kind of reality in the past or in the future. We live, as August Comte said, dead men's lives, encased in our pasts, but this is especially so in prison when we try to find some sustenance for our starved and locked-up emotions in memory of the past or fancies of the future.
– Pandit Nehru, *The Discovery of India*

Part Three

A Wind of Change
(1976 to 1981)

THE UPRISING OF SOUTH AFRICAN youth in Soweto on 16 June 1976, against being taught in Afrikaans, sparked a fierce response from police resulting in hundreds of deaths and many more people leaving South Africa for clandestine military training. But the inmates of Robben Island only got to hear of what had happened in August that year when a new prisoner, Eric Molobi arrived. The news he brought made up for their lack of newspapers and radios. It was at once exhilarating and depressing. A new resistance to apartheid was growing in the country, unleashing a vicious reaction from the regime, but at the same time, it steeled an angry generation for the armed struggle ahead. It brought the veteran inmates a sign that their ideal of liberation might indeed be within reach.

The uprising resulted in a fresh crop of Robben Island prisoners, referred to by the veterans as the 'Post-Soweto chaps'. They arrived "very angry, impatient, and determined to pursue the fight violently," recalls Kathrada. The Rivonia men had to calm them down and persuade them of the futility of their desire to assault the warders. Many of them consequently took up studies and stopped their battles with the prison officials. Kathrada and his colleagues grew to learn much from these prisoners and forged solid friendships with many of them.

The year 1977 saw the end of hard labour for prisoners. A new commanding officer in 1978, lightened up on the draconian rules and allowed prisoners to listen to SABC radio. For the first time in 12 years, they had beds on which to sleep.

What is this, the sound and rumour? What is this
that all men hear,
Like the wind in hollow valleys when the storm is
drawing near,
Like the rolling on of ocean in the eventide
of fear?
'Tis the people marching on.
Whither go they and where come they? What are
them of whom ye tell?
In what country are they dwelling 'twixt the gates
of heaven and hell?
Are they thine or mine for money? Will they serve
a master well?
Still the rumour's marching on.
O ye rich men, hear and tremble! For with words
the sound is rife:
"Once for you and death we laboured; changed
henceforward is the strife.
"We are men, and we shall battle for the world of
men and life,
And our host is marching on."
Hark the rolling of the thunder!
Lo, the sun! and lo, thereunder
Riseth wrath and hope, and wonder,
And the host comes marching on.
– William Morris, *The March of the Workers*

He who does not believe in miracles is no realist.
– Christian Morgenstern (*German poet*)

If you're still living, never say never.
What is certain isn't certain.
Things will not stay as they are …and
Never becomes Before the Day is Out.
– Bertold Brecht, *In Praise of Dialectus*

Prudent! In times like these, when terror makes might seem right, there is a higher duty than prudence.
– Edith Cavell

History does nothing, possesses no enormous wealth, fights no battles. It is rather man, the real, living man, who does everything, possesses, fights. It is not 'History', as if she were a person apart, who uses men as a means to work out her purposes, but history itself is nothing but the activity of men pursuing their purposes.
– Karl M *[Marx]*

We must see the first images which the external word casts upon the dark mirror of his mind; or must hear the first words which awaken the sleeping powers of thought and stand by his earliest efforts, if we would understand the prejudices, the habits, and the passions that will rule his life. The entire man is, so to speak, to be found in the cradle of the child.

– Alexis de Tocqueville

How can it be? How can it be that truth engenders hatred? … It is because it is so well loved that those very men who love something that is opposed to it claim that something is truth. And, as they hate being wrong, they hate him who wishes to convince them of their error. Thus what they believe to be the truth makes them hate the truth itself.

– St Augustine, Bishop of Hipponius, 'Confession' (*taken from 'My Secret Diary of the Dreyfus Case' 1894 – 1899, Maurice Paleologue*)

Bliss was it in that dawn to be alive.
But to be young was very Heaven!
– Wordsworth, *Prelude*

Attack, attack! Keep at their heels! Attaquez
donc toujours!
– Frederick of Prussia

That which we are, we are ... made weak by time
and fate, but strong in will to strive, to seek, to
find, and not to yield.
– Alfred Lord Tennyson, *Ulysses*

We shall never surrender, and even if, which I do
not for a moment believe, this island or a large
part were subjugated and starving, then our
Empire beyond the seas, armed and guarded by
the British fleet, would carry on the struggle, until,
in God's good time, the new world, with all its
power and might, steps forth to the rescue and
liberation of the old.
– Winston Churchill, *[speech to the House of
   Commons, 4 June, 1940]*

The day is coming, not in the far future, but in
near, when Taal-speaking and English-speaking
South Africans will stand shoulder to shoulder
guarding the rights of the land which is theirs.
And, when that day comes, the first steps will have
been taken towards the realisation of that for
which we labour and for what we want – a South
Africa, not mighty in wealth nor in number, but
great in freedom, not merely in freedom from
external control and interference, but in that
deeper and much more important internal form of
freedom which gives to every man and woman in
the land, irrespective of race or sex or speech or
colour, the largest amount of liberty and justice
accorded to men and women anywhere.
– Olive Schreiner (*in a letter to the 'Cape Times'*
  10 May 1905)

The greatness of today is built on the efforts of
past centuries. A nation is not contained in a day
nor in an epoch, but in the succession of all days,
all periods, all her twilights and all her dawns.
– Jean Jaures

Offtimes the test of courage becomes rather to live than to die.
– Vittorio Alfieri

Mistakes are inevitable – no human being is perfect. The important thing is not to make no mistakes, but to make only few and small mistakes and to learn from them.
– Vladimir Illych *[Lenin]*

How does Man live? By throttling grinding, sweating
His fellows, and devouring all he can!
His one chance of survival's in forgetting
Most thoroughly that he himself's a man.
No, gentlemen, this truth we cannot shirk:
Man lives exclusively by dirty work.
– Bertold Brecht, *Threepenny Novel (based on John Gray's Beggars' Opera, written 200 years ago)*

The triumph of wicked men is always short lived.
– Honore de Balzac, *The Black Sheep*

News, like substances, ought to be divided into
solids, fluids and gasses – and appropriately
labelled as such for publication.
– Sydney Harris, *Readers' Digest*

But those who have no pennies
O, what do they do, pray?
Lie down and get themselves buried
While the world goes its way?
O no, for we'd have no pounds, then,
If they were allowed to do that!
For without their toiling and moiling
We'd none of us grow fat.
(Nursery rhyme)

Give me leave, before I sit down, to call on you
to drink our Sovereign's health: The Majesty of
the People.
– *(Toast proposed by the Duke of Norfolk at a banquet
to celebrate the birthday of Fox, prominent anti-
monarchist and friend of the French Revolution.)*

It is not a question of who's going to throw the first stone. It's a question of who's going to start building with it.
– Sloan Wilson, (*Readers Digest*)

"You are two branches of one tree; you are the sons of one mother. Is this goodly land not wide enough for you, that you should rend each other's flesh at the bidding of those who will wet their beaks in both your vitals?"
– Olive Schreiner (*pleas for justice towards the 'Bantu' and tolerance and love towards fellow men, from 'Trooper Peter Halket of Mashonaland' in 'Portrait of a South African Woman'*)

Great works are performed not by strength but by perseverance.
– Samuel Johnson

There is a great man who makes every man feel small. But the real great man is the man who makes every man feel great.
– Charles Dickens

Time in its irresistible and ceaseless flow carries
along a flood of all created things and drowns
them in the depths of obscurity... But the tale of
history forms a very strong bulwark against the
stream of time, and checks in some measure its
irresistible flow, so that, of all things done in it, as
many as history has taken over it secures and binds
together and does not allow them to slip away into
the abyss of oblivion.
– Anna Comnena

It is to the credit of human nature that, except
where its selfishness is brought into play, it loves
more readily than it hates. Hatred, by a gradual
and quiet process, will even be transferred to love,
unless the change be impeded by a continually
new irritation of the original feeling of hostility.
– Nathaniel Hawthorne, *The Scarlett Letter*

My nature is to join in love, not hate.
– Sophocles, *Antigone*

Sow flowers, and flowers will blossom
Around you wherever you go;
Sow weeds, and of weeds reap the harvest,
You'll reap whatever you sow.

> You'll reap whatever you sow, …
> The harvest is certainly coming:
> You'll reap whatever you sow.

Sow blessings and blessings will ripen:
Sow hatred, and hatred will grow:
Sow mercy, and reap sweet compassion:
You'll reap whatsoever you sow.

Sow love, and its sweetness uprising
Shall fill all your heart with its glow;
Sow hope, and receive it fruition:
You'll reap whatsoever you sow.
– Hymn No 191, *Alexander's Hymn*

So long as we love we serve,
So long as we are loved by
others I would almost say we are indispensable;
and no man is useless while he has a friend.
– Robert Louis Stevenson

To do good is noble; to teach others to do good is nobler, and no trouble.
– Mark Twain

Our remote ancestors were not impressive creatures; they cut a poor figure among the great beasts of the forest. They had no huge claws and teeth, no scaly armour, no wings, no great turn of speed, not even the power of rapid reproduction. But they had one miraculous trick – they could adapt themselves to make the best of changing conditions; they were flexible and experimented. Now that we have conquered – and heavily ruined – the earth, now when we change our conditions at often appalling speed and almost blindly, we are in sore need of all the adaptability our species can still discover in itself. We must think freshly, think fast, improvise, experiment, and be tolerant of one another's mistakes. Despair and hate are not going to help us.
– J.B. Priestly, *Essays of Five Decades*

The most wasted of days is that on which one has not laughed.
– Nicolas-Sebastien Chamfort

I can trace my ancestry back to a protoplasmic primordial atomic globule. Consequently, my family pride is something inconceivable. I can't help it.
– W.S. Gilbert

A traitor is a traitor – no need to understand any further. And a system which rests all its weight on a piece of treachery makes the treachery not only inevitable, but sacred.
– D.H. Lawrence, *Aaron's Rod*

Art has an enemy called ignorance.
– Tuscan adage

It is so nice to lie here and hear that noise ... I like to feel that strange life beating up against me. I like to realize forms of life utterly unlike mine, when my own life feels small, and I am oppressed with it, I like to crush together, and see it in a picture in an instant, a multitude of disconnected unlike phases of human life – a medieval monk

with his string of beads pacing the quiet orchard,
and looking up from the grass at his feet to the
heavy fruit trees; a little Malay boy playing naked
on a shining sea-bach; a Hindu philosopher alone
under his banyan tree, thinking, thinking,
thinking, so that in the thought of God he may
lose himself
– Olive Schreiner, *The Story of An African Farm*

Democracy is the way to give the people the
greatest illusion of power while allowing the
smallest amount in reality.
– Walter Bagehot, *The English Constitution*

Of all the vulgar modes of escaping from the
consideration of the effect of social and moral
influences upon the human mind, the most vulgar
is that of attributing the diversities of conduct and
character to inherent differences.
– J.S. Mill

I get up early, winter and summer, to partake of the sacrament of daybreak. The pleasure of the habit is at its most exquisite round about the springtime of the year. There is something in the air before the dawn, even a wet and cloudy dawn; which is pristine, crystalline. But there is no word for it, especially if the dawn be a clear one, with the sky rinsed and swept in preparation for the casting of the shafts of light up and over out of the eastern rim of the universe.
– R. Church (*Readers Digest April 1972*)

The extremes of passion look silly when written.
– Stendahl

Verba volent, Scriptis manent. (*The spoken word flees; the written word remains*)
– Ancient Roman adage

To sing, to laugh, to dream
To walk in my own way and be alone,
Free, with an eye to see things as they are,
A voice that means manhood – to cock my hat
where I choose – At a word, a Yes, a No,

To fight – or write. To travel any road
under the sun, under the stars, nor doubt
if fame or fortune lie beyond the bourne –
Never to make a line I have not heard
in my own heart; yet, with all modesty
To say: "My soul be satisfied with flowers,
with fruit, with weeds even; but gather them
in the one garden you may call your own."
So, when I win some triumph, by some chance,
Render no share to Caesar – in a word,
I am too proud to be a parasite.
– Edmond Rostand, *Cyrano de Bergerac*

A lovely home atmosphere is one of the flowers of
the world, than which there is nothing more
tender, nothing more delicate, nothing more
calculated to make strong and just the natures
cradled and nourished within it. Those who have
never experienced such a beneficent influence will
not understand wherefore the tear springs
glistening to the eyelids at some strange breath in
lovely music. The mystic chords which bind and
thrill the heart of the nation, they will never know.
– Theodore Dreiser, *Sister Carrie*

(Peter Ustinov explains why he reads so much:) "If you're going to be the prisoner of your own mind, the least you can do is to make sure it's well furnished."

There is so much good in the worst of us,
And so much bad in the rest of us,
That it hardly becomes any of us,
To talk about the rest of us.
– *Farmers' Weekly*

Part Four

Freedom is coming
(1982 to 1989)

MANDELA, SISULU, MHLABA, AND MLANGENI were transferred to Pollsmoor Prison on the mainland in March 1982. Seven months later, with a few hours notice, Kathrada was able to say goodbye to his comrades in B Section, including Mbeki and Motsoaledi who remained on the Island. At Pollsmoor each man subscribed to a different newspaper. The news they got from the media and from visits, was of impending freedom in South Africa.

The resistance to apartheid rose to its highest point in the 1980s, followed by fierce crackdowns by a state bolstered by successive States of Emergency. Anti-apartheid forces were making great strides, but they paid enormous prices: tens of thousands were detained without trial; activists in neighbouring states were attacked and scores were murdered both inside and outside South Africa, and judicial executions were at an all-time high.

Yet the struggle outside prison walls signalled real hope for the Rivonia Trialists. "The UDF is there, Cosatu is there, demonstrations are taking place, so it would have had an effect on me," said Kathrada about the more positive tone emerging in his notebooks.

President P.W. Botha's January 1985 offer to release political prisoners, if they renounced violence, was refused.

Later that year Mandela was separated from his comrades and asked them not to protest. It emerged that he had taken the first steps towards negotiating with the apartheid government. At the time Kathrada was dead against talking to the enemy, but soon accepted that he was wrong.

In 1986, the Rivonia Trialists were allowed, for the first time, contact visits, to have a television set, wear wrist watches, write poetry and keep pets.

Things fall apart: the centre cannot hold
Mere anarchy is loosed upon the world
The blood-dimmed tide is loosed
and everywhere
The ceremony of innocence is drowned.
The best lack all conviction, while the worst
Are full of passionate intensity.
– W. B. Yeats, *The Second Coming*

The crisis persists precisely because the old is dying
and the new cannot be born. In this interregnum a
great deal of morbid symptoms appear.
– Antonio Gramsci

No day dawns for the slave, nor is it looked for. It
is all night – night forever.
– Jermain Loguen (*1818-1872. Fugitive son of a
slave master and a slave woman*)

You come from afar … But what does distance
mean to your blood, which sings without borders:
Death may call your name any day;
who knows where, in what cities, fields or roads?
whether it be this country, or that, whether it be
large or small,
whether it be coloured pastel on the map.
The people spring from the same roots, the
same dream.
Anonymous, speaking simply, you have come.
You don't even know the colour of the walls
in homes you have pledged to guard.
The earth now covering you is what you loved.
Ready for battle, accepting the bullet of death.
Stay – the trees, the plains wish it,
The particles of light that radiate
From the one song the sea roars out: Brothers!
Madrid grows greater and brightens with
your name.
– Alberti (*on the men of the International Brigade*)

A soldier without politics is an assassin.
– Samora Machel

Herriet Tubman, former slave, played a great part in
helping slaves to freedom, after she herself escaped. She
inspired the Underground Railroad. She is said to have
led 300 to freedom, after 15 journeys.
– *National Geographic July 1984*

War is the father of all and king of all
Some he shows as gods, others as men
Some he makes slaves, others free.
– Heraclites, *The Cosmic Fragments*

When bad men combine, the good must associate;
else they will fall one by one.
– Edmund Burke (*18th Century British conservative*)

For the family, sacrifice the individual,
For the community, the family;
For the country, the community;
For the soul, all the world.
– Rabindranath Tagore (*From the flypage of Ezekiel*
Mphahlele's autobiography, 'Afrika My Music
1957 – 1983')

The corpses of young men
Those martyrs that hang from the gibbets – those
hearts pierced by the gray lead.
Cold and motionless as they seem, live
elsewhere with unslaughter'd vitality.
They live in other young men, O kings!
They live in brothers, again ready to defy you!
– Walt Whitman

… it is sufficient for evil to succeed for good men
to remain silent …
– Edmund Burke

When one considers the human race, it often
seems a pity that Noah didn't miss the boat.
– Mark Twain

Politics is the name of tragedy.
– Napoleon Bonaparte

The people's flag is deepest red,
It shrouded oft our martyr'd dead
And ere their limbs grew stiff and cold,
Their hearts' blood dyed its ev'ry fold.

Chorus

Then raise the scarlet standard high,
Within its shade we'll live and die,
The cowards flinch and traitors sneer,
We'll keep the red flag flying here.

It well recalls the triumph past;
It gives the hope of peace at last;
The banner bright, the symbol plain,
of human rights and human gain.

Chorus

With heads uncovered swear we all
And bear it onward till we fall.
Come dungeon dark or gallows grim,
The song shall be our party hymn.
– In *Die Burger*, 16 June 1984 *[words by
Jim Connell]*

The only obligation which I have the right to
assume is to do at any time what I think right ...
I know this well, that if one thousand, if one
hundred, if ten men whom I could name – if ten
honest men only, as, if one HONEST man, in this
state of Massachusettes, ceasing to hold slaves,
were actually to withdraw from this co-partnership
(with the government) and be locked up in the
county jail therefore, it would be the abolition of
slavery in America.
– Henry David Thoreau

Terror on this war-darkened morn,
Alarm bells suddenly shrill;
A child looks up like a frightened fawn,
Somehow it doesn't seem real.
The sudden chatter of gunfire,
The deadly whine of a bomb,
The walls crash down in the bloodstained mire,
Then the final, despairing cry.
Farewell little one ...
– Marion Sparg, (*13 years, Std 6, Cambridge High,*
   East London, magazine)

[Marion Sparg later joined Umkhonto weSizwe, the armed wing of the African National Congress, and in 1986 was convicted of treason. She served four-and-a-half years of a 25-year jail term.]

Patria Libre o Morir. (*A free homeland or death – Sandinista slogan*)

Do what you must, come what may.
– Leo Tolstoy (*as he lay dying*)

An event has happened upon which it is difficult to speak and impossible to be silent.
– Edmund Burke

Nothing is shameful except to have no shame.
– Blaise Pascal

Die Kind
By Ingrid Jonker

Die kind is nie dood nie
die kind lig sy vuiste teen sy moeder
wat Afrika skreeu skreeu die geur
van vryheid en heide
in die lokasies van die omsingelende hart.

Die kind lig sy vuiste teen sy vader
in die optog van die generasies
wat Afrika skreeu skreeu die geur
van geregtigheid en bloed
in die strate van sy gewapende trots.

Die kind is nie dood nie
nóg by Langa nóg by Nyanga
nóg by Orlando nóg by Sharpeville
nóg by die poliesiestasie in Phillipi
waar hy lê met a koeël deur sy kop.

Die kind is die skaduwee van die soldate
op wage met gewere sarasene en knuppels
die kind is teenwoordig by alle vergaderings en
wetgewings
die kind loer deur die vensters van huise en die
harte van moeders

die kind wat net wou speel in the son by
Nyanga is orals
die kind wat 'n man geword het trek deur die
ganse Afrika
die kind wat 'n reus geword het reis deur die
hele wereld

sonder 'n pas.

– From 'Rapport' newspaper, 28 February 1988
[Ingrid Jonker, who died in 1965 at the age of 31,
wrote this poem in response to the 1960 Sharpeville
massacre in which 69 people protesting the pass laws
were shot dead by police, many in the back.
Nelson Mandela read an English translation of this
poem at the opening of the first sitting of South
Africa's democratic parliament in May 1994.]

Jedem das seine (*To each what he deserves*
– sign outside Buchenwald)

Boeke is bomme: vir my dooie broer, Tiro
daar was n swartman sy naam was Tiro, Abraham
(en Tiro lê in sy eie bloed)
hy wou most geleerdheid gaan haal uit 'n
"universiteit"
(en Tiro lê in sy eie bloed)
waar hy hardegat geword hê tom sy opvoeding töe
te pas
(en Tiro lê in sy eie bloed)
en voor hy nog verban kon word tot die staat van
leefdooies
het hy sy geboortegrond verlaat
vir 'n dorp met die naam Gaberones in 'n land
met die naam van Botswana in die woestyn
met oral vlammetjies van n stryd-om-vryheid
wat sy woorde laat ontbrand het ...
en die baas moes toon dat n kaffer
sy plek moet ken, of so nie ...
en die baas het vir Tiro n boek gepos
en Tiro lê in sy eie bloed
en Tiro lê in sy eie bloed
en Tiro is die binnevlam binne die rooi vlam.
– Breyten Breytenbach (*Rapport 28 Feb 1985*)

[Breyten Breytenbach was sentenced to nine years in prison for High Treason in 1975 and was held at Pollsmoor Prison. Kathrada was there for a short while before Breytenbach was released in 1982. Abraham Tiro, a leader of the South African Students Organization was killed by a parcel bomb in Botswana in 1974.]

... I have a dream that one day this nation will rise up and live out the true meaning of its creed, 'we hold these truths to be self-evident, that all men are created equal.' I have a dream that one day on the red hills of Georgia, sons of former slaves and the sons of former slave owners will be able to sit down together at the table of brotherhood ... I have a dream that my four little children will one day live in a nation, when they will not be judged by the colour of their skins, but the content of their character.

– Dr Martin Luther King (*at Lincoln Memorial Washington D.C. at a rally of 25 000 on 28 August 1963*)

When I saw them
I nearly wept.
Young and handsome
sons of Africa.
Full of love
Their faces could tell.
Mzondeleli, with a
loving smile.
Mthetheleli, seemingly
Deep in thought.
I refused to believe it,
They are going to
hang!
Oh! Sons of Africa!
Freedom lovers
Lovers of mankind.
For the dream they had.
They will be hanged.
For hatred of seeing
men in bondage
They will be hanged.
For hatred of seeing
their fathers.
Mothers, Sisters.
Brothers and Lovers

oppressed and exploitated
They will be hanged.
Oh! Sons of Africa!
Your blood shall
nurture
The tree of Freedom
One day your dream,
our dream;
The dream of the oppressed.
Will come TRUE.
– S.B. Jayiya, *Ezibeleni (City Press 22 May 1988)*

When lilacs last in the dooryard bloom'd,
And the great star droop'd in the western sky in
the night,
I mourn'd, and yet shall mourn with
ever-returning spring.
Ever-returning spring, trinity sure to me
you bring,
Lilac blooming perennial and drooping star in
the west
And thought of him I love.
– Walt Whitman (*threnody on the death of Lincoln.
Threnody: (song of) lamentation on death*)

Revolution is an idea which possesses bayonets.
– Mussolini

In the dark times
Will there also be singing?
Yes, there will also be singing
about the dark times.
– Bertold Brecht

We must carry on as though we are immortal,
even in the face of death.
– Peter Abraham, *The View from Coyoba*

One owes respect to the living; but to the dead
one owes nothing but the truth.
– Voltaire

Call no man fortunate until he is dead.
– Euripides

Wars cannot be won by bullets but only by
bleeding hearts.
– Mahatma Gandhi

They first came for the Communists, and I did not
speak because I was not a Communist.
Then they came for the Jews, and I did not speak
because I was not a Jew.
Then they came for the trade unionists, and I did
not speak because I was not a trade unionist.
Then they came for the Catholics and I did not
speak because I was a Protestant.
Then they came for me and by that time there was
no one left to speak.
– Pastor Martin Niemoller (*1939*)

When some men plot, good men must plan
When some men burn and bomb, good men must
build and bind.
When some men see ugly words of hatred, good
men must commit themselves to the glories
of love.

When some men would seek to perpetuate an
unjust status quo,
Good men must seek to bring into being a real
order of justice.
– American pacifist

A nation and a woman are not forgiven the
unguarded hour in which the first adventurer that
came along could violate them.
– *18ᵗʰ Brumaire [of Louis Napoleon, by Karl Marx]*

There is no struggle
from which women are exempt,
no struggle in which women
do not play their part;
our struggle is in fact
for women's day,
to struggle for tomorrow
in a women's fight today

There is no freedom
while women are not free,

no freedom when women
do not have their say;
freedom day in fact
is women's day,
freedom day tomorrow
is women free. Today.
– from 'Women's Day Song'
  (*International Women's Day 8 March*)

Where there is discord, may we bring harmony.
Where there is error, may we bring truth. Where
there is doubt may we bring faith. Where there is
danger, may we bring hope.
– St Francis of Assisi

The spirit of truth and the spirit of freedom they
are the pillars of society.
– Hendrik Ibsen, *1828 – 1906*

AHMED KATHRADA

for fatima
so much love

>they have taken you away
>and left you untouched
>they have locked you up
>and set you free
>they have silenced your voice
>and proclaimed your message

i raked rock with my fingers
battered my head to bone
for a long time lay senseless
heart shocked to stone

then words of the Quran
stirred within me
i breathed again
knowing you were safe

>'Had was caused this Quran to descend
>upon a mountain, verily (O Muhammad)
>you would have seen it humbled
>torn apart by the fear of Allah.'

you too accepted the weight of the Quran
of undefiled, unconquerable truth

of many-faceted, all-encompassing,
overwhelming love
for the whole of mankind.

you too assumed, undaunted, that awesome trust
fulfilled steadfastly that formidable task
of being the eyes of the nation
the heart, the blood, the pulse of your fellow man

those who are trying to subdue you
would achieve success a million times greater
if they concentrated all their effort
on moving mere mountains.

– Shabbir Banoobhai, *Echoes of my other self*
  (Ravan 1980)
  [This poem was written in 1976 at the time of the
  Soweto uprising, in honour of Fatima Meer. Mrs
  Meer, who was in police detention at the time, is a
  close friend of Kathrada.]

To be ignorant of what occurred before you were
born is to remain always a child.
– Cicero *46BC*

Schreibt und farschreibt. *Write and record. The doyen of Jewish historians, Simon Dubnov, 81, shouted these words as he was shot in the back by a Gestapo officer who had been one of his pupils.*

I tell you naught for your comfort, yea, naught for your desire, save that the sky grows darker yet, and the sea rises higher.
– G.K. Chesterton, *Ballad of the White Horse*

I am a selfish man, as selfish as any man can be. But in me somehow or other, so it happens, selfishness has taken the form of benevolence.
– Jeremy Bentham

It is a dry white season
dark leaves don't last, their brief lives dry out
and with a broken heart they dive down gently
headed for the earth
not even bleeding.
It is a dry white season brother,

only the trees know the pain as they still
stand erect
dry like steel, their branches dry like wire,
indeed, it is a dry white season
but seasons come to pass.
– Mongane Wally Serote

Pity the nation divided into fragments, each
fragment feeling itself a nation.
– Khalil Gibran (*Lebanese Poet*)

Physicians have been pouring drugs about which
they know little, for diseases about which they
know less, into human beings about whom they
know nothing.
– Voltaire

Tomorrow's sun shall rise ... and it shall flood
these dark kopjes with light and the rivers shall
glint in it ... And I say to you that even here, in
the land where now we stand, where today the

cries of the wounded and the curses of revenge ring in the air; even here, in this land where man creeps on his belly to wound his fellow in the dark, and when an acre of gold is worth a thousand souls, and a reef of shining dirt is worth half a people ... even here that day shall come. I tell you, Peter Simon Halket, that here on the spot where now we stand shall be raised a temple. Man shall not gather in it to worship that which divides; but they shall stand in it shoulder to shoulder, white man with black, and the stranger with the inhabitant of the land; and the plan shall be holy...
– Olive Schreiner, *Trooper Peter Halket (Quoted by Menan du Plessis in her speech, on the occasion and presentation of the Olive Schreiner Prize (of the English Academy) for her novel, 'A State of Fear'. She donated her R500 prize to the UDF. Cape Times 10/4/1986.)*

He whose wisdom brings him into power needs goodness to secure that power. Else, though he get it, he will certainly lose it.
– Confucius *551 – 479 BC*

Happiness is the only good:
The time to be happy is now
The place to be happy is here
The way to be happy is to make
other people happy.
– Robert Green Ingersoll

Laughter is the shortest distance between
two people.
– Anon

Thy sins and hairs may no man equal call
For, as thy sins increase, thy hairs do fall.
– John Donne, *A Licentious Person*

A man, I suppose, fights only when he hopes,
when he has a vision of order, when he feels
strongly there is some connection between the
earth on which he walks and himself.
– V.S. Naipul, *The Mimic Man*

Russia is strong because she has lots of birch trees.
– Dostoyevsky, *The Brothers Karamazou.* *(Birch is used for flogging peasants and offenders.)*

Tenderness for what a child is, and respect for what he may become.
– Louis Pasteur

Only innocence dares to be so bold. Both vice and virtue (when it has acquired some knowledge) weigh their actions carefully.
– Honore de Balzac, *Eugenie Grandet*

"Do you know which is the greatest gift of all to cultivate?" …
"Shall I tell you? The child's eye, that's the great art. Seeing things as though for the first time. Perceiving everything, always, as though it were brand new in the world. As though you had never seen it before."
– Lionel Abrahams, *The Celibacy of Felix Greenspan*

A Coloured *[sic]* is a very frightened-to-death Afro-American. A negro is one that makes it in the system, and he wants to be white. A nigger, he's loud and boisterous, wants to be seen. Nobody likes a nigger. A black man has pride. He wants to build, he wants to make his race mean something. Wants to have a culture and art forms. And he's not prejudiced. I am a black American man. Now you go ahead and print it.
– James Brown, *the godfather of soul talking to Dave Hill of the 'London Observer'. James Brown born 1933, composer of 'Say it Loud, I'm Black and I'm Proud' in 1968.*

The most wasted of days is that on which one has not laughed.
– Nicolas de Chamfort

To be without some of the things you want is an indispensable part of happiness.
– Bertrand Russell

Ek is swart gebore. Op skool was ek swart. As ek siek is, is ek swart. Swart sal ek doodgaan.
Maar jy witman! Jy was pienk toe jy gebore is, wit toe jy skool toe is, bloedrooi as jy skaam, bruin as jy in die son gelê het, en blou van die koue. Jy skrik jou asvaal en stamp jou pimple in pers ... En jy het die vermetelheid om vir my gekleurd te noem.
– *(Graffitti on Cape Town wall, Pollux Rapport, 26 July 1986)*

Life is full of choices, but you never get any.
– Charlie Brown (*and Linus, Lucy, Snoopy, etc. Created by Charles Schultz*)

It is better to remain silent and be thought a fool, than to speak out and remove all doubt.
– Abraham Lincoln

The 40s are the old age of youth. The 50s are the youth of old age.
– Victor Hugo

And it never enters anyone's head that to admit a greatness not commensurate with the standard of right and wrong is merely to admit one's own nothingness and immeasurable littleness.
– Leo Tolstoy

Those who love generously are loved in return.
– Chinese maxim

Sisulu – By Don Mattera

> The man
> The wife
> The family…

Restless seagulls sweep over Island – Pollsmoor
echoing the shouts of our bonded nation
singing the songs of waiting
Sisulu:

> The man
> The family
> The pain of sacrifice

We salute you again and yet again
Patriarch of liberation

We greet you Albertina
Matriarch of Martyrs
your tears nourish our dreams
your courage irons our wills

We salute the Family
the sons and the daughters
when commitment lights the tree of Freedom
and Justice and Human Love

Albertina:

> The mother
> The agony
> The sacrifice

Though silenced you speak
within Sechaba's soul
carrying the burden
paying the price

The unspoken fervour of admiration
burns our eyes

we salute you Sisulu:

> The Giving Tree
> The unbroken seed
> The impending victory

Bayete!
(Written especially for the Indicator's Newsmaker of the Year Award to the Sisulu family)

Men use thought only to justify their injustices,
and speech only to camouflage these things.
– Voltaire

Nobody knows what kind of government it is who
has never been in prison.
– Leo Tolstoy

I know this day will pass,
This day will pass,
That one day, some day,
The dim sun with tender smiling
will look in my face
Looking his last farewell,
Beside the way, the flute will sound.
The kine will graze on the river-bank
The children will play in the courtyards,
The birds will sing.
Yet this day will pass,
This day will pass.
– Rabindranath Tagore (*Anthology of Modern Indian
   Poetry, London 1927*)

The word 'negotiate' was first used in recorded time by Shakespeare in 1599 in *Much Ado About Nothing*. – "Let the eye negotiate for itself, and trust no agent." The root of the word is two Latin terms meaning "without ease".
– Prof Geoff Hughes (*Wits*), '*Sunday Star*' *Review 30 July 1989*

A prison taint was on everything there. The imprisoned air, the imprisoned light, the imprisoned clamps, the imprisoned men, were all deteriorated by confinement. All the captive men were faded and haggard, so the iron was rusty, the stone was slimy, the wood was rotten, the air was faint, the light was dim. Like a well, like a vault, like a tomb. The prison had no knowledge of the brightness outside; and would have kept its polluted atmosphere intact, in one of the spice islands of the Indian Ocean.
– Charles Dickens, *Little Dorrit*

A poor peace is better than a good quarrel.
– Russian proverb

Neem raad aan van die man wat twyfel, want die
ander man het die saak net van die een kant
bekom.
– C.J. Langenhoven

We know what happens to people who stay in the
middle of the road. They get run over.
– Aneurin Bevan

"Don't you realise? – discussion, dialogue, call it
what you will is the one thing they dare not allow.
For once they start allowing you to ask questions
they're forced to admit the very probability of
doubt. And their raison d'etre derives from the
exclusion of that possibility."
"Why must it be so?" I asked.
"Because it's a matter of power. Naked power.
That's what brought them there and keeps them
there. And power has a way of becoming an end in
itself..." ..."Once you have your bank account in
Switzerland, and your game farm in Paraguay, and
your villa in France, and your contacts in
Hamburg and Bonn and Tokyo – once a flick of
your wrist can decide the fate of others – you need

a very active conscience to start acting against your own interests. And a conscience doesn't stand up to much heat or cold, it's a delicate sort of plant."
– André Brink, *A Dry White Season*

In order to become a dragon a chameleon must pass a very rigorous examination.
– Chinese proverb

Two roads diverged in a wood, and I –
I took the one less travelled by
And that has made all the difference.
– Robert Frost, *The Road Not Taken*

Nothing that happens is ever as bad as one fears or as good as one hopes.
– Theodore Herzl

No one can be perfectly free until all are free;
No one can be perfectly moral 'till all are moral;
No one can be perfectly happy 'till all are happy.
– Herbert Spence

You should never have your best trousers on when you turn out to fight for freedom and truth.
– Henrik Ibsen

It was the best of times, it was the worst of times, it was the age of wisdom, it was the age of foolishness, it was the epoch of belief, it was the epoch of incredulity, it was the season of Light, it was the season of Darkness, it was the spring of hope, it was the winter of despair, we had everything before us, we had nothing before us …
– Charles Dickens, *A Tale of Two Cities*

One crowded hour of glorious life is worth an age without a name.
– Thomas Osbert Mordaunt

Time does not console, it effaces.
– Guizot

An old man going on
a lone highway
Came, at the evening, cold and grey,
To a chasm vast and deep and wide,
The old man crossed in the twilight dim,
The sullen stream had no fear for him;
But he turned when safe on the other side
And built a bridge to span the tide.
"Old man," said a fellow pilgrim near,
"You are wasting your strength with building here;
"Your journey will end with the ending day,
"You never again will pass this way;
"You've crossed the chasm, deep and wide,
"Why build this bridge at evening tide?"
The builder lifted his old grey head;
"Good friend, in the path I have come," he said.
"There followed after me today
"A youth whose feet must pass this way.
"This chasm that has been as naught to me
"To that fair-haired youth may a pitfall be;
"He too must cross in the twilight dim;
"Good friend, I am building this bridge for him!"
– (*Unknown origin. Found among the papers of the
late humorist and artist of the 'Star', Ken Smith.
Published in the 'Star' 25/10/1985*)

When the gods wish to punish us they answer
our prayers.
– Oscar Wilde

Go in search of your people.
Love them;
Learn from them:
Serve them:
Begin with what they have
Build on what they know

But the best leaders
when their task is accomplished.
their work is done
The people all remark
We have done it ourselves.
– *(from SAHWCO publication)*

It is good to be back among one's countrymen
because one knows when they're lying.
– Rudyard Kipling

The most important thing in the Olympic Games is not to win but to take part, just as the most important thing in life is not the triumph but the struggle. The essential thing is not to have conquered but to have fought well.

– Baron de Coubertyn, *First President of the International Olympic Committee 1896 – 1925*

My desire is to make what haste I can to be gone.

– Oliver Cromwell

Ahmed Kathrada, Walter Sisulu, Elias Motsoaledi and Andrew Mlangeni were transferred to Diepkloof Prison in Soweto on 13 October 1989, and freed on 15 October. Raymond Mhlaba was sent home to Port Elizabeth. Govan Mbeki had been released on 5 November 1987. The ANC, South African Communist Party, PAC and other organisations were unbanned on 2 February 1990. A week later, Nelson Mandela was also released from prison. He became South Africa's first democractically elected President on 10 May 1994. Kathrada served as a Member of Parliament and

President Mandela's parliamentary counsellor until 1999, when both men retired from Parliament. Robben Island Maximum Security Prison became a museum and was declared a World Heritage Site. Kathrada was chairperson of the Robben Island Museum Council from 1997 to 2005.

Rest in Peace

Four of the Rivonia Trialists have since passed away:

Elias Motsoaledi (aged 69, on the day Nelson
   Mandela became President, in 1994)
Govan Mbeki (aged 91, in 2001)
Walter Sisulu (aged 90, in 2003)
Raymond Mhlaba (aged 85, in 2005)

Acknowledgements

Kimberley Worthington thought of making this book while she was researching *Ahmed Kathrada: Memoirs*. She passed it on to me due to the intervention of other projects in her life (not least the imminent arrival of her and Henry's first baby). Despite his punishing schedule, Ahmed Kathrada was constantly available to offer advice and to answer endless questions, with genuine interest and great humour. My husband Claude Colart was, as always, unwaveringly supportive, and offered his own valuable and critical insights. Maggie Davey and Chris Cocks of Jacana Media made it all come together. Thank you to Shawn Paikin, for the design; Kira Schlesinger, for her sharp eye; and Wim Vos, for his advice on copyright. Thank you to Isu Chiba for his foreword; Themba Hadebe for his photograph; to Anthony Akerman for his contacts, and to Verne Harris and Anthea Josias of the Nelson Mandela Foundation for their assistance. Thank you to Victor Houliston for his advice on the Greek texts.

My deep gratitude goes to the South African writers quoted in this collection, and particularly those who, without hesitation, gave their personal permission for their work to be included. They are: Antjie Krog, Don Mattera, Marion Sparg, Breyten Breytenbach, Mongane Serote, and Shabbir Banoobhai. Despite numerous efforts, I was unable to trace S.B. Jayiya of Ezibeleni for his moving poem about the execution of freedom fighters, which Kathy copied into his notebook from *City Press* newspaper.

Special acknowledgement is made to the following for their financial support of this project: Dr Jakes Gerwel; Eddie Daniels; André Odendaal, Linda Hill and Roger Breitbart; Anthony Sampson; Ben and Jean Shek and family; Tommy and Dela Vassen; Lord Joel Joffe; Dr Nikolai Mortenson; Leonie Walker and Kate O'Hanlan; Anne Schneller and Michael Bratton; Ursula and Bob Vassen; Sharon Gelman and Artists for a New South Africa; Dr Marcellette (Marcie) Gay Williams; Alexandra Paul; C. Kurt Dewhurst, Marit Dewhurst and Marsha MacDowell; Sheila and Nontsikelelo Sisulu and family; Mark Kornbluh and Mimi Behar; John and Joan Eadie; David Wiley and Christine Root; Chuck and Anne Korr, University of Missouri, St Louis; Nesha Haniff, University of Michigan; Larry and Judy Kendall; Donna Katzin, Anna Cecila

Blackshaw, Tim McKee and Rio Mandela Blackshaw McKee; Dr Ivan May, in memory of another Gentle Man and Gentleman: Xolani Dyusha (1961 – 1999).

With grateful thanks to all the copyright holders for their permission to publish these extracts. In particular I would like to thank Seamus Cashman, Catherine Trippett and Naomi Tummons who went far beyond the call of duty in assisting me to find other copyright holders.

The extract from *The View from Coyoba* by Peter Abraham, is reprinted by permission of New Africa Books.

The extract from *Waiting for Godot* by Samuel Beckett is reproduced by permission of Macmillan Ltd.

The extracts from Bertold Brecht's works, *Caucasian Chalk Circles, Threepenny Opera* and *In Praise of Dialectus* are reproduced by permission of Methuen Publishing Ltd.

The extract from *A Dry White Season* by André Brink, published by Minnerva, is reprinted by permission of The Random House Group Ltd.

The extract from *Pavilion of Women* by Pearl Buck, is reprinted by permission of A.P. Watt Ltd. on behalf of The Estate of Pearl S. Buck.

The extract from *Gitanjali* by Rabindranath Tagore, is published by permission of The National Book Trust of India.

The extract from *The Lost World of the Kalahari* by Laurens van der Post, published by Chatto & Windus is reprinted by permission of The Random House Group Ltd.

The extract from *Spartacus* by Howard Fast, was reproduced by permission of PFD (www.pfd.co.uk).

Various sources were consulted in the production of this book. They include:

Conversations with Ahmed Kathrada.

Ahmed Kathrada's unpublished secret prison notebooks.

Letters from Robben Island: A Selection of Ahmed Kathrada's Prison Correspondence 1964-1989. Edited by Robert D. Vassen, (Mayibuye Books and Michigan State University Press 1999).

Ahmed Kathrada: Memoirs. By Ahmed Kathrada, (Zebra Press 2004).

There and Back: Robben Island 1964-1979. By Eddie Daniels, (Mayibuye Books 1998).

Bram Fischer: Afrikaner Revolutionary. By Stephen Clingman, (David Philip Publishers and Mayibuye Books 1998).

Long Walk to Freedom. By Nelson Mandela,
(Macdonald Purnell 1994).
Walter & Albertina Sisulu: In Our Lifetime. By
Elinor Sisulu, (David Phillip Publishers 2002).
Mandela: The Authorised Biography. By Anthony
Sampson, (HarperCollins 1999).

Every attempt has been made to contact the
copyright holders of the material published here
and the editor and publishers welcome corrections
to the copyright information currently available.